regaining JOY

Overcoming Stress and Sadness

Renee Bartkowski

Liguori
LIGUORI, MISSOURI

Imprimi Potest:
Thomas D. Picton, C.Ss.R.
Provincial, Denver Province
The Redemptorists

ISBN: 978-0-7648-1580-5
© 2007, Liguori Publications
Printed in the United States of America
07 08 09 10 11 5 4 3 2 1

Scripture quotations are from the *New Revised Standard Version of the Bible,* © 1989 by the Division of Christian Education of the National Council of Churches of Christ in the USA. Used with permission. All rights reserved.

Liguori Publications, a nonprofit corporation, is an apostolate of the Redemptorists. To learn more about the Redemptorists, visit Redemptorists.com.

To order, call 1-800-325-9521
www.liguori.org

Table of Contents

Introduction

DO YOU EVER feel like you're drowning in a pool of unexplainable sadness? Do you experience periods of deep depression from time to time—or is there perhaps a steady persistent undercurrent of sadness and joylessness in most of your days?

Many of us don't realize that there are various degrees of depression ranging from being actually clinically depressed to simply being chronically sad and joyless. And in today's stress-driven world, it's often difficult to hold on to a joy-filled approach to life.

People who are clinically depressed usually need both professional counseling and drug therapy to relieve their depression. Antidepressants have been quite successful in alleviating the imbalance of chemicals in the minds of depressed individuals, but they ordinarily do not have the power to change the patterns of thinking that lead most people into sadness and depression in the first place.

Almost anyone can easily fall into a depressed way of living if our thinking and attitudes have become so negative and distorted that we actually lose our ability to feel joy. We must change our way of thinking in order to escape the possibility of becoming victims of joyless living.

The purpose of this book is to help us bring the ability to feel joy back into our lives through the use of down-to-earth, mind-changing prayer-conversations with our Lord. The prayers and suggested practices in this book will not only help bring more contentment into our daily lives, but can help us develop a closer relationship with our Lord by making him a partner in our quest for joy.

Opting for Optimism

My Understanding

LORD, I KNOW that it's not always possible to control our feelings, because feelings have a way of rushing in and depositing themselves in our psyches even before we realize that they're there. Emotions such as anger, jealousy, and fear often barge right in and take over—whether we want them to or not.

None of us likes the fact, Lord, that we don't always have the power to choose the exact emotions that we'd like to feel—or that we think we ought to feel. But we can console ourselves with the knowledge that there's something we do have the power to choose, for we all have the power to choose our attitudes—the way we view and respond to the events in our lives. And in this, the choice is completely ours, isn't it, Lord? We have the option of deciding just how we want to face life whether we want to face it in a positive and optimistic manner or in a discouraged, disillusioned, or negative mode.

We have to admit, Lord, that for those of us who don't have a naturally optimistic personality, it's rather hard to respond to some of the difficult and more depressing things in our lives with a positive attitude. It's hard to keep our spirits up when our spouses or children disappoint us, when serious illness or troubling problems overtake us, when relationships and marriages end and our hearts are broken. But we don't have to allow things such as these to totally devastate us. It is definitely

1

possible to live through them without falling into despair. Of course, having faith in your help and in your teachings makes it all easier.

We have to keep reminding ourselves that we actually do possess the power to choose a more optimistic outlook on life. All that is needed is our willingness to choose it. But let us realize that this isn't a choice that should be made only once. It's a choice that must be made over and over again, day after day. It's a choice that requires a lot of open-mindedness, a lot of determination, and a lot of practice.

My Prayer

Dear Lord, I'm definitely willing to try to be a more optimistic person.

There's an old song that tells us "to always look for the silver lining and (we) will find the sunny side of life." Lord, I do want my life to be sunnier and more joyful. I do want to develop a more positive, more joy-filled outlook on life. But if I don't actively and deliberately search for the good side of things, I most likely will not find it. So I promise, Lord, to make a determined effort to look for the positive side in everything that happens each day.

I have to admit that I've spent a good part of my life focusing on the negative. When something bad happens, I usually immediately jump to the conclusion that this one event will undermine everything else that's happening in my life and that if things are bad now, they will most certainly get worse.

I remember the day when my husband came home and told me he had lost his job. I immediately went into a tailspin of fear and depression. All I could focus on was our inability to pay our bills and the eventual loss of our home. Instead of offering him my support, I exhibited a lack of faith in him that could have dragged him right down with me. Thank goodness he's a much more optimistic person than I am, for he was not only able to console me, but was eventually able to find a job he liked even more. And none of my fears ever actually materialized.

Teach me, Lord, how to approach my daily life in a more positive manner. I've noticed that people who are optimists are usually able to roll with the punches and quickly get beyond the disappointing things that happen to them. They don't dwell on them as I often do. Let me learn to think as they do, Lord, to just shrug off disappointments as unfortunate events that will soon pass. Let me learn to have faith that they will eventually be resolved and I will be able to look forward once again to better times.

Teach me, Lord, how to find the good in everything. The Bible says that "all things work together for good for those who love God" (Romans 8:28). It does not claim that all things will be good, but it implies that some good often comes out of the bad things that happen to us. Yes, losing a job can be a devastating experience, but how many times do you hear of it leading to a better paying, more enjoyable job. I guess it's true, Lord, that in life, one door closes and another door opens.

Help me to use the wisdom that you offer me, to learn how to find and focus on the good. Let me learn how to view life with a brighter, more open, more optimistic outlook.

My Resolutions

Lord, I will make a special effort to fill my mind with a steady diet of positive thoughts. Every time a pessimistic mindset overtakes me, I will do everything I can to push it away by replacing it with thoughts that are optimistic. I will make it a point to search for something good in everything. And when I find it, I will focus all my attention on it.

I will also develop the habit of using positive imaging, Lord. Whenever I face a difficult situation, I will take the time to fill my mind with images that lead to positive results. I've read about successful baseball players who visualize a home run in their minds whenever they step up to bat. I've heard of professional golfers who, before they tee off, hold a picture in their minds of the golf ball going straight down the middle of the fairway. I've read about cancer survivors who spend time each day picturing their tumor cells shrinking and dying while undergoing chemotherapy. Remind me, Lord, to make use of this powerful way of thinking each time I face a challenge.

Putting Perfection in Its Place

My Understanding

LORD, I KNOW that we have to stop expecting life to be perfect, for real life is definitely not perfect or easy or fair. But that's life! I guess we must learn to accept life as it is, not as we would like it to be. We have no choice but to deal with all its problems, all its inequalities and ups and downs. So it isn't what we thought it would be! So what! So we'd better get over it! Isn't that right, Lord?

I guess it takes a lot of good and bad, exhilarating and disappointing, successful and unsuccessful things to round out a meaningful life. Life never just flows smoothly and neatly from one good event to another. In fact, it often seems that as soon as we draw up a plan to have our lives progress in a certain perfect way, it usually takes no time at all for us to be shown that life just isn't going to cooperate with our preconceived notions. We make plans to take a vacation and our spouse gets too sick to travel. We have dreams of our son going to a particular college and he doesn't get accepted. The company we work for goes bankrupt and we lose our job. We buy a new home and we get transferred to another city.

It seems that our lives are being constantly interrupted by sickness, unexpected problems, breakdowns, lack of time, lack of funds, mistakes, and accidents. We tend to impatiently regard all these things as detours that just don't belong on the road of life. But looking back, we can see that the road of life is never perfectly straight. It's made up more of winding detours than it is of straight and direct routes.

Getting through these winding byways is really what life is all about, isn't it, Lord? We must deal with all the challenging detours while trying to keep our lives moving in the right direction. Certainly not an easy road map, is it, Lord? But not an impossible one to follow. Not one that should be resented or judged as unfair. We all have our detours to contend with, don't we?

Our lives would be easier if we could just convince ourselves that things are not perfect and that is not necessarily bad. Most things in life are not all bad or all good. Sometimes something that is only partially successful can be considered satisfying and good. We should never hesitate to give ourselves credit for these partial successes, should we?

Let us learn, Lord, how to avoid becoming disappointed if all our hopes and dreams don't turn out as we expected them to.

My Prayer

Lord, I refuse to let myself keep falling into this "trap of perfectionism" that I have fashioned for myself. I will learn to accept life as it is with all its imperfections, all its annoyances, and detours. You have placed us in an imperfect world, a world with storms and accidents and diseases and conflicts. You knew that life in this world would not be a bed of roses.

So let me learn to accept that fact and stop expecting perfection from it.

Lord, there are times when I wear myself out trying to make things perfect. And when things don't turn out exactly as I think they should, I get discouraged and begin feeling like a failure.

Teach me, Lord, how to turn my thinking around. Let me realize that I do not have to do things perfectly. All that is needed is that I do the best I can. Let me learn how to give myself credit, not just for actually succeeding, but for trying to succeed.

Looking back, Lord, I can see that I always wanted to wait until things were perfect before I allowed myself to enjoy them. I remember the many years I spent mistakenly believing that when my children were finally in school, life would be easier and more enjoyable. I also recall thinking that when I got my house remodeled exactly the way I wanted it, my life would finally be ideal. It's a waste of time to approach life in this way. I must learn to lighten up and enjoy my life whenever and wherever I can, in between all the imperfect and sometimes frustrating events that occur each day. With your help, Lord, I will do just that.

My Resolutions

Lord, I will take the time to enjoy and treasure every accomplishment in my life, no matter how small, how complete or incomplete it may be.

Dear Lord, I will stop feeling dissatisfied with how much I can or cannot accomplish each day. Many of us usually make lists of things that must get done. From now on, instead of focusing on the tasks I can't get to, I will take the time to pat myself on the back for those I was able to get done.

When things go wrong and my detours get to be depressing, I will remind myself that I can probably learn more from the detours than I can from the straight road. With your help, Lord, I will learn how to put perfection in its place.

Appreciating Our Assets

My Understanding

LORD, WE KNOW life on this earth is not perfect, nor can we expect perfection from ourselves or others. But that knowledge doesn't usually stop us from getting down on ourselves because of our imperfections. Instead of giving ourselves credit for all our accomplishments, we focus on weaknesses and limitations and end up feeling totally dissatisfied with ourselves.

We'd all like to be better looking, thinner, stronger, smarter, more athletic, and more talented. We compare ourselves to other people. When we come up short, we get depressed.

Let us realize, Lord, we're not really that different from most other people. We all have our own share of faults and weaknesses. Some of us have trouble controlling our tempers. Some of us are shy, short on confidence, or have a hard time making friends. Some of us are clumsy and lack athletic skills. There are those of us who are uncomfortable with the way we look.

Remind us, Lord, that only self-centered people are completely satisfied with everything about themselves. It was never your intention for us to feel devastated by our limitations. Nor do you ever want us to feel devastated by our failures or the mistakes that we all often make. When you created us, you knew we would make mistakes. That's why you offered us forgiveness. And if you, our God, can forgive us for our poor judgment, how can we possibly refuse to forgive ourselves?

Let us realize, Lord, that when we do understand our limitations, then maybe we'll be able to face life with a more contented outlook.

My Prayer

Lord, help me overcome my need for perfection that leads to depression and disappointment. Teach me how to accept and love myself as I am—with all my warts and weaknesses. Only you are perfect, help me do good. And don't let me ever forget to take the time to recognize and really appreciate all the assets and talents that you have blessed me with.

Whenever I begin to feel disillusioned with myself, remind me, Lord, that you always have, and always will, love me unconditionally. I know you expect me to work on my faults, but you would never withhold your love for me because of these faults. You love and accept me just the way I am and expect me to have the same love and acceptance for myself as you do, for you created me the way I am, and everything you create is good.

I know, Lord, that there's a good reason you wanted me here like I am, right now, at this time, in this place. Even though I am imperfect and have many faults, I know you can use me to serve you and others just as I am.

I also know that when you created me, you did not abandon me. Creation is an ongoing process for all of us. You will continue to create and mold me all through my life. Allow me to be open to your plan of creation for me, Lord, with a positive and trusting attitude. Teach me how to look forward eagerly and expectantly to what I can become in the future.

Whenever I happen to feel dissatisfied with myself or my accomplishments, let me remember, Lord, that not all of us were given the talent to do great things. Most of us are destined to live ordinary lives. But ordinary certainly doesn't mean insignificant, does it, Lord? There are some people who end up being celebrities, starring in the movies or on the Broadway stage or professional athletes, earning millions of dollars. There are famous journalists and statesmen who shape the course of history. But there are also those ordinary, but magnificent people who spend their lives waiting on tables, repairing cars, or cleaning houses, struggling to make their children's lives better than theirs.

Let me realize, Lord, that as long as I use whatever talents you have given me to the best of the ability, I am living a meaningful life, a life that is deemed good in your eyes. I should never hesitate to give myself credit for that.

Keep reminding me, Lord, that no wise person ever loves every little thing about himself. Let me learn to be proud of that which is good and strong and loving in me. Dear Lord, if you can love me as I am, how can I possibly dare not to love myself?

My Resolutions

Each day, Lord, I will tell myself that no one is perfect except you. Instead of wasting my time obsessing about my weaknesses, I will spend time focusing on and being grateful for my assets.

Whenever I begin to feel dissatisfied with my accomplishments, Lord, I will direct my attention away from what I can't do, and toward what I can do. I'll become my own little cheering section for each and every thing that I accomplish each day. Whenever I make a mistake, I will remind myself that everyone makes mistakes. You want us all to follow your example, Lord, and quickly forgive ourselves, just as you always forgive us. I will remember that you never asked us to be perfect; you asked us to be loving.

Developing an Attitude of Gratitude

My Understanding

LORD, IT'S ALMOST impossible to feel depressed when you feel grateful. It seems that gratitude and depression are totally incompatible. It makes sense for us to try to develop a good, strong "attitude of gratitude."

The problem is we're usually so busy dealing with all our daily activities and responsibilities we never think of taking time to acknowledge the good things we have in our lives.

Lord, I read about a psychological study that said people who make a habit of counting their blessings can actually improve both their mental and physical health. College students who took part in this study were asked to take a few minutes each day to actually write down their blessings. After a few weeks, the students found that they felt more optimistic, more enthusiastic, and more satisfied with their lives and their relationships. The chronically ill people, who also took part in this study, reported that they worried less, slept better, and generally felt more healthy and content.

It would be great, Lord, if we could experience this healing power of gratitude. Perhaps if we could train ourselves to refrain from complaining about all that's wrong with our lives, it would be easier for us to remember that our lives include a lot of good things for which we should be deeply and constantly grateful.

My Prayer

Dear Lord, forgive me for taking my blessings for granted. Forgive me for forgetting to express my thanks to you.

I often get so wrapped up in thinking about all the tedious chores and worrisome problems and challenges I have to deal with that I'm not aware that I have so many good things in my life, too. I focus on the fact that my children need too much care, my aging parents need too much help, that there's never enough time to properly finish the endless projects I must accomplish at work. Always too much to do and too little time. It's exhausting.

Whenever I start feeling down about all that is wrong with my life, remind me to stop my negative thinking and take a moment to consider my blessings. There are so many ordinary things in my life that I just don't think to appreciate—my family and friends who give me love and support, my comfortable home, the food I eat, the good fortune of living in a nation that is more secure and peaceful than most other nations.

Let me remember, Lord, there are millions of people in this world of ours who are not fortunate enough to enjoy things that I often take for granted. When do I ever think of expressing my gratitude for the ability I have to walk, to hear music, to see a beautiful sunset? How often do I remember to feel grateful that I have running water, electricity, and conveniences that make my life easier and more comfortable? Sometimes I wonder how can I dare to be so ungrateful.

Do I ever question if I deserve to have all that I have, while some people have so little? I think of the homeless people in our own city, the starving children in Third World countries.

Are they any less deserving than I am? Am I, with my lack of gratitude, at all deserving?

Let me remind myself, Lord, that the blessings I possess are gifts that you have chosen to give me. It is you who have placed me here in this life, in this place, with these blessings, not because I deserve them, but because you have chosen to allow me to have them. I could have been born someplace else, in a war-torn or famine-ravaged country. I could have been born handicapped or blind or deaf.

Don't let me ever be so ungrateful that I fail to acknowledge your goodness. Let me feel thankful for every little thing in my life. Let me remember to express my gratitude and make it an important part of my daily living.

My Resolutions

Lord, I will make it a practice to wake up each morning giving thanks to you for the new day, for the opportunity to serve you and your people. I forget that this is the reason why I'm here, isn't it, Lord?

Each night when I go to bed, I will take a few minutes to think about all the good things that happened during the day and I will say a special prayer of thanks to you, Lord. I will begin to keep a list of my blessings. Each day I will dig deep into my mind to find three things for which I am thankful and I will write them down. Whenever I'm feeling low, I'll take out my list of blessings and read them.

I will try to learn how to be grateful for even the not-so-nice things that happen in my life. I can at least thank you, Lord, for helping me through these difficult times. I will also try to find some meaning in them, something that will teach me to be a stronger, better, a more appreciative person.

Putting the Past in the Past

My Understanding

MANY OF US, LORD, live too much in the past, rehashing in our minds all the things that have gone wrong in our lives. We dwell not only on the past, but on the worst of the past. We have a need to beat ourselves over the head with all the "what-could-have-beens" in our lives. As a result, we keep ourselves stuck in our pain.

How many hours do we spend thinking about the opportunities we've missed, the jobs we didn't get, the promotions that went to someone else? How many times do we go over the mistakes we've made, the failures we've experienced, the arguments we regret having had? It's obvious, Lord, that when we immerse ourselves in these negative memories, it stirs up all the bad emotions that the original situation brought on. Our bodies are overwhelmed with all the same feelings—the frustration, the hurt, the anger, the embarrassment—that they felt when all those unpleasant things were actually happening. Subjecting our bodies to those emotions over and over again is not only unhealthy, it's also depressing. Why do we do it? Why do we make ourselves feel bad?

The Bible tells us to forget those things that are behind us (Philippians 3:13–14). It says simply to admit that we are not perfect, to forgive ourselves for any mistakes we have made, and to just get on with our lives.

My Prayer

Help me, Lord, to take your advice to put the past in the past, to simply let go of bad memories and troubled feelings and get my life moving forward again. I know that I wasted too much time trying to figure out why things happened as they did, what I could have done differently to avoid bad situations—and on and on.

Remind me, Lord, that sometimes there are no satisfactory explanations for why things happen as they do. In this imperfect world, they often happen just because they happen. People get sick. They get involved in accidents. They are victims of damaging storms and floods. Because each of us is imperfect, it's almost impossible to totally avoid making wrong decisions. I can remember the regrets I had when I invested a much-needed sum of money very unwisely and lost it. And another time when I was offered two jobs and I chose the one that turned out to be too stressful.

I guess I have to keep remembering, Lord, that I can't fix or change past mistakes by constantly worrying about them. Don't let me go on continuously blaming myself for something I did—or failed to do—in the past. Don't let me allow myself to be bullied by guilt.

Let me realize that my life will be much easier and more pleasant if I can more willingly embrace the concept of "forgiving and forgetting" and give up my habit of dwelling on the past. Teach me, Lord, how to live my life more fully in the present.

My Resolutions

Whenever I begin thinking about past mistakes, Lord, I will convince myself that I had done the best I could with what I knew and felt at that time. I will give myself credit for at least recognizing the fact that I do resort to poor judgment at times. I will simply forgive myself, try to improve, and quickly move on.

With your guidance, Lord, I will be smart enough to protect my health by refusing to subject my mind and body to the unhealthy, mentally, and physically damaging emotions brought on by rehashing of past mistakes, hurts, and failures. I will distract myself from these emotions by putting on some uplifting music and immediately getting busy with something that I enjoy doing or at least don't mind doing.

Facing the Future With Faith

My Understanding

I KNOW, LORD, that having a "what-if" mentality can be extremely exhausting and intimidating. Seldom do negative people think of all the nice things that may happen in the future. They ordinarily zero in on the things that go wrong, wearing themselves out with worry.

We all know that the act of worrying can never, in itself, make things better, but we worry anyway, unwisely and uselessly wasting our time and our strength. For many of us, worry becomes a habit that is extremely hard to break. Not only does it often make us actually afraid of the future, it also shows us how lacking in faith we are.

The Bible tells us that you, Lord, do not allow a trial in our lives that is too great for us to bear (1 Corinthians 10:13). It also tells us that you send us strength when we need it.

But you know how fearful and untrusting we can be, Lord. We usually feel totally insecure when we don't possess the strength we need ahead of time. We spend hours stressing over the belief that, since we feel weak and unconfident today, it's just not possible for us to be strong and confident enough to handle the problems and challenges that are coming tomorrow.

But you don't usually waste time giving us strength, do you, Lord? The Bible shows us how you tested the faith of the Israelites when you gave them manna from heaven while they were out in the desert. You wanted them to gather enough nourishment for just one day at a time and to trust in your promise that you would send them more when they needed it. So, too, you want us to show our faith in you by believing that you will send us help when we need it. We must learn to confidently step out in faith, to trust that you will send us tomorrow's strength tomorrow.

Many of us marvel at how we managed to get through some of the challenges that we previously swore we could never possibly survive. With your help, we did get through them, didn't we, Lord? Remind us to think of those times whenever we're tempted to start worrying.

My Prayer

Dear Lord, help me break my habit of worrying about the future. Let me be able to view my worrying for what it actually is—a complete waste of time and energy. This tendency to worry is so ingrained in me that I often worry not only about the things that are going to happen in the future, but also about things that might happen.

I've heard it said that about sixty percent of what we worry about never actually happens. I remember worrying about a presentation that I had to give. I spent two whole weeks in a state of tortured anxiety, certain that I would be too nervous to speak. After making myself sick with worry, I ended up managing to give an informative and surprisingly relaxed presentation. Another time I became completely stressed out when a storm knocked out the power. I spent five anxious hours worrying that our inactivated sump pump would cause our basement to flood. All the worry was for nothing, the power was restored and everything turned out fine.

I guess Mark Twain was quite right when he said, "The worst things in my life never happened." What do I accomplish by spending so much time worrying about the future? All I seem to do is upset myself. What a useless, unproductive, and disturbing pastime that is!

With your help, Lord, I will avoid worrying about future problems. I will keep reminding myself to live in the present. I'll keep working to develop a strong faith in your promise to give me the strength I need for tomorrow when tomorrow finally comes.

My Resolutions

Alcoholics Anonymous has a "24-hour plan" that teaches its members to focus on keeping sober one day at a time. I will use this concept, Lord, to teach myself how to live in the present, how to focus on getting through one day at a time, one single day, day by day, hour by hour.

When I find myself worrying about tomorrow, I will say a prayer acknowledging my faith in you, Lord. I will trust in you to give me the strength and help that I need. I promise, Lord, to make an effort to get rid of my negative "what-if" mentality by replacing it with an attitude that anticipates a good and positive outcome.

Jousting With Jealousy

My Understanding

IF THERE'S ONE EMOTION that has the power to make us feel really bad, it's jealousy. Jealousy is a big-time joy blocker, isn't it, Lord? It's like a piece of rough sandpaper that grates against us, slowly grinding away at our happiness. It has the ability to make us feel totally dissatisfied and discontented. We can actually feel sick with envy.

But it's very hard for many of us to keep that green-eyed monster from creeping in and out of our lives. We notice things about other people, things that they have that we'd also like to have—a nicer home, a newer car, a vacation condo in the Caribbean. We notice the exciting things other people are doing—spending weekends on the lake in their boat, golfing, and partying at their country club. We envy the things that they can afford—and we immediately think, "Some people have all the luck! Why aren't we as lucky as they are?" We become dissatisfied and depressed.

We waste time wanting someone else's luck—someone else's life—even though we don't really know how good or how bad their life actually is. Despite their seemingly good fortune, their lives may be much harder and unhappier than ours. Even the rich and famous suffer with depression, commit suicide, and escape into drugs or alcohol to deaden their pain.

So why do some of us spend so much time making ourselves miserable with envy? It just doesn't make sense, does it, Lord?

My Prayer

Help me, Lord, to rid myself of that green-eyed monster that takes over my life. Let me realize that I don't really need all the material possessions that my friends and neighbors have for me to feel contented and satisfied.

I'd feel better if I'd just stop comparing myself to people who have more than I have or who have an easier life than I do. Keep reminding me, Lord, that satisfaction and contentment are relative concepts. I have blessings that millions of other less fortunate people do not have, blessings for which I should be grateful, but, sad to say, I don't always show that gratitude.

I know, Lord, that there are people who are happier than others. There are those who seem content and at peace when things are going wrong. Instead of envying them, I should try to find out how they remain contented. Lord, it is me who makes the choice to be jealous, and it's a choice that I can avoid. With your help, Lord, I will learn to be more satisfied and content, and certainly more grateful for all that I do have.

My Resolutions

Lord, I will stop thinking about people who are better off than I am. I know there are people who are better looking, more talented, richer, and smarter than I am. There will always be people who lead more interesting and exciting lives than I do. I will stop comparing myself to them and try to be more satisfied with my assets, my talents, and all the good things that exist in my life. With your help, Lord, I will succeed.

I will remind myself that I can actually choose to be jealous or choose not to be jealous. It's up to me, isn't it, Lord? Whenever a jealous thought begins to hound me, I will push it away by thinking about and expressing my gratitude for the many blessings I do possess, blessings that other people would be extremely grateful to have.

Relinquishing Resentment

My Understanding

ANGER IS ANOTHER huge joy blocker, another big depression builder, isn't it, Lord?

How can we possibly feel peaceful and contented when we are filled with disturbing and irritating feelings of anger and resentment? Not only does anger make us feel bad, it's probably one of the most physically damaging emotions we can experience.

All we need do is spend time thinking about someone we resent—a friend who has hurt us, a co-worker who has wronged us, a boss who treats us unfairly—and our bodies can get so stressed and exhausted that our immune systems can be weakened.

It's so easy, Lord, to become angry, to stubbornly hang on to our resentments—much easier than it is to forgive and forget. But being human, we take the easy way out and sometimes nurse our anger. We spend weeks not speaking to a brother. We refuse to cooperate with a co-worker. We vengefully spread gossip about a neighbor. Or we just let our anger build up quietly inside of us. We turn it over and over in our minds instead of simply acknowledging it and releasing it.

Remind us, Lord, that holding our anger in or constantly thinking about it not only hurts us, it can bring our lives to a standstill. We become so engrossed in being angry that we no longer have the energy or the incentive to move forward. We become imprisoned by our anger.

We must also remember that anger can put up a barrier between us and you, Lord. You have told us to forgive those who anger us, just as you offer forgiveness. Teach us how to be more forgiving.

Let us never forget, Lord, that anger doesn't hurt the object of one's anger as much as it hurts the person who harbors it. We make ourselves miserable by keeping ourselves in a state of heightened irritation, while the person who is the cause of that irritation is totally oblivious to our distress. Our anger at a co-worker who gets promoted over us can bring on days of misery. Meanwhile, the co-worker goes on to enjoy his good fortune unaware of the disappointment this promotion has caused. We feel we have the right to be angry, but our anger doesn't usually repair the damage. Life is often unfair, and subjecting ourselves to that much useless stress just doesn't make sense, does it, Lord?

My Prayer

Dear Lord, help me to learn how to control my anger. There's a part of me that sometimes feels that I have a right to stay angry when someone has wronged me. There's a stubborn streak in me that doesn't want to give up my resentments and my feelings of vengefulness.

There are times when I like to blame others for things that go wrong in my life, when I feel justified in placing the blame on someone else for my unhappiness. At times, I even blame you, Lord, for making my life hard and miserable. There are those moments when I get angry at myself for making stupid mistakes that leave me feeling foolish, frustrated, and angry.

This is not a wise approach to life, is it, Lord? The one I'm hurting the most with all this anger is me, isn't it?

Teach me, Lord, how to let go of anger, resentment, and vengefulness, and to do it quickly. Help me learn how to forgive others for their thoughtlessness and mistakes. I remember a time when I wasn't invited to a party while most of my friends had been invited. I was not only hurt, I was angry and didn't try to hide my resentment. I later learned that the friend who was extending the invitation had mistakenly been told that I'd be out of town that weekend. Mistakes are made by all of us, and hurtful things are also often done unintentionally, with no thought of malice. Let me learn to excuse others for their thoughtlessness.

Forgiveness is a must in everyone's life and the faster I am able to forgive, the faster I'll rid myself of anger's damaging stress. Lord, help me not to take my anger and frustrations out on others. I usually take my angry feelings out on those closest and most dear to me, though they have nothing to do with the cause of my anger. I recall how the problems I had at work resulted in my coming home and getting into an argument with my husband. How many times did my anger at being stuck in traffic prod me into becoming impatient with my children? Remind me of how illogical and unfair this type of behavior is.

Dear Lord, let me realize how incompatible anger is with contentment and happiness. Help me rid myself of this harmful emotion and learn to be more forgiving, more understanding, and more compassionate.

My Resolutions

I will remind myself, Lord, that I always have the choice of responding to the disturbing things that happen in my life with either anger and resentment or forgiveness and understanding. I will remember that it is totally my choice and that I'm responsible for making a choice that is both wise and kind.

Dear Lord, when someone does something that annoys me and makes me angry, I will immediately remind myself that I, too, often slip up and do things that are annoying to others. I will not waste my time stressing myself over people who do ignorant and uncaring things. I will follow your teaching, Lord, to forgive others as you forgive us and to forgive myself as you forgive me.

Dealing With Disappointment

My Understanding

LORD, YOU NEVER PROMISED to eliminate our problems and disappointments. You merely assured us that you would always stay near us and help us get through them. But why do some of us have such an extremely hard time dealing with disappointment?

It would be easier if we could just accept the fact that setbacks are simply a normal part of everyone's life. We could accept them better if we could convince ourselves that they can have a positive effect on us and our attitudes. Failing a test may make us try harder next time. It could lead to better study and work habits that will benefit us the rest of our lives.

Many people find that we learn more from our disappointments than we do from our successes. It takes a lot of disappointment, failure, and pain to teach us how to become more accepting, more persevering, and stronger individuals. We would never appreciate our successes quite as much if we had never experienced failure and disappointment. Isn't that true, Lord?

I know, dear Lord, you are always willing to teach, to mold, and to continue to create us. We must allow you to work in us, mustn't we, Lord? We must leave ourselves open to the lessons you want us to learn even if those lessons turn out to be tough and painful.

There isn't a person alive who hasn't experienced disappointment throughout their lives. There are women who can't conceive a child, men who can't find decent jobs, wives who are abandoned by their husbands, parents whose children get involved with drugs, people who lose their homes and their loved ones. Young children face disappointments. The people who seem to weather them the best are usually those who possess the deepest faith in your promise to stand by us and support us.

I ask you, Lord, to help those of us who are wobbly in our faith to learn how to firmly and confidently trust that you will always be at our side to help us deal with our disappointments.

My Prayer

Lord, I've always had a hard time accepting failures as a normal part of life. I sometimes react to them with so much resentment, loss of confidence, and self-pity that I don't leave room for your strength and wisdom to get through. I put so many obstacles in your path that I block out the help you want to give. I'm one of those people who tends to ask, "Why me, Lord?" instead of "Why not me?"

Teach me, Lord, to accept disappointment as a natural part of life. Help me learn how to avoid feeling so despondent when certain situations turn disappointing. Help me to stop dwelling on all the unhappy events of my life. I keep looking back to all the short stories I wrote that never got published, to all the relationships that failed to last, to all the promises that were made to me that were never fulfilled and I get depressed.

I don't want to feel that life is treating me unfairly. Instead of wasting my time feeling bad, help me learn from life's down times, help me improve my character and my approach to life.

Remind me, Lord, that my batting average at success and failure is probably just as good as anyone else's. Let me accept the good and bad with equal grace. Don't let me be tempted to allow failure and disappointment to bring me to a standstill filled with self-pity and despair. Teach me how to get on with my life, knowing that you are always there to help me as long as I remember to ask for your help.

My Resolutions

Lord, you promised to deliver us through hard times, not from them. I will remember that you are constantly trying to give me the strength and wisdom that I need to help me "hang in there." I will be open to accepting your strength and wisdom.

When I'm faced with a disappointing event, I promise, Lord, that I will think about it only as long as it takes me to find a lesson in it. I will put it out of my mind and not beat myself down with regrets. I will avoid talking about my disappointments and will try to steer conversations to more uplifting and entertaining subjects.

I will regard each setback, each failure, each painful disappointment as a gentle nudge prodding me forward to meet and successfully face the next challenge. Lord, I will give myself credit for being able to get through my disappointments, and will grow stronger and wiser as a result of them.

Surrendering Self-Pity

My Understanding

LORD, I'VE NOTICED depressed people get offended if someone even suggests they may be feeling sorry for themselves. Many individuals who feel sad and depressed either go into complete denial or they regard themselves as innocent victims caught in a trap through no fault of their own.

Some people rationalize that if they are overwhelmed by self-pity, it's because they have a good reason to feel sorry for themselves. They forget that just about everyone has reason to feel sorry for themselves.

If we are honest with ourselves, most of us would have to admit that we do wallow in a bit of self-pity from time to time. The trouble is some of us wallow in it much too long. We don't want to give up the comfortable little self-pitying cocoons that we have spun for ourselves. So we stay snugly nestled in them, so engrossed in feeling sorry for ourselves that we can't possibly see a way out.

When life gets too difficult, it is easier to remain in the pity pit than it is to try to force ourselves to tough it out. But taking the easy way out works against us, doesn't it, Lord? Like quicksand, our self-pity makes us sink deeper and deeper into a swamp of sadness until it becomes almost impossible for us to pull ourselves out. But with your help, Lord, it's not impossible for us to do so, is it? Not as long as we're at least willing to shed those encompassing cocoons of ours.

My Prayer

Lord, I remember a time, when I was deeply depressed. I could not see that I was feeling sorry for myself, let alone admit to it. Even my prayers reflected this attitude. They focused exclusively on how hard and unfair and sad my life was.

But with medication, supportive people, and the help you gave me, Lord, I was finally able to acknowledge that this was a significant part of what was holding me in the grip of depression. It was this admission that made it possible for me to slowly climb out of my darkness.

A lot of very difficult, depressing, and frightening things happened that made me believe that I deserved to feel sorry for myself: my cancer, the loss of my brother, the devastating illness that incapacitated my husband, the long decline of my aging parents, and finally the loss of my parents. I thought I had a lot of reasons to feel sorry for myself. But I could also see that my self-pity played a large roll in keeping me enslaved in sadness and immobile. The only way to break the bond that held me was to want to break it.

Give me the strength I need, Lord, to keep me from sinking into that trap again. There are hundreds of thousands of people worse off than I am. I know some people whose lives are much harder, much more difficult, and much sadder than mine and they have not fallen prey to self-pity.

Lord, life is a series of challenges, a series of struggles. We can either deal with them and work our way through them or we can refuse to face them, give up, and fall into despair. I often think of my cousin whose wife is suffering with Alzheimer's, of my friend who just lost a child in a car accident, and of my neighbor whose teenaged daughter has run away from home. I see them all courageously facing their daily challenges, not allowing their grief and sadness to push them into a well of self-pity.

Give me the wisdom I need, Lord, to know that I, too, can avoid this crippling emotion. Give me the strength to avoid it.

My Resolutions

Dear Lord, I will be aware of the danger signs of self-pity and not to give in to them. The minute I start feeling sorry for myself, I will begin counting my blessings. I will focus—with gratitude—on the good things in my life. Instead of thinking of myself as "poor me," I will look at the reasons why I should feel fortunate.

I will remind myself, Lord, that it takes two steps to stay away from self-pity. First, I must admit that I'm feeling sorry for myself. Second, I must acknowledge the fact that it takes a decision to avoid becoming entrapped in this time-wasting and depressing attitude.

Saying 'No' to Negativity

My Understanding

LIFE IS MADE UP of all kinds of experiences, isn't it, Lord? Some good. Some bad. People who survive the negative experiences are usually those who don't let them get the better of them. They avoid focusing on them and choose not to let these things take over their lives.

On the other hand, there are those of us who habitually focus on the bad things and often blow them totally out of proportion. We zero in on the worst possible end results and tend to let a single negative incident cause us to get depressed. Some of us are so overly sensitive that all it takes is the criticism of one person to make us feel that we will be ostracized by everyone. Some of us are so negative that we just automatically respond to any challenge by immediately saying, "No, I can't do that"—even before we give ourselves time to really think it through. What a self-defeating way to live!

Dear Lord, I've read that we become what we think, and if we continually entertain negative views and attitudes, we can't help but become very pessimistic and depressed individuals. It seems that anyone, even those not prone to depression, can become depressed if they spend their days filling their minds with negative thoughts.

If we believe we have the power to refuse to get bogged down with negative attitudes, then I guess we have to be willing to work at ridding our minds of our sad and negative thoughts. Perhaps when we finally make up our minds to do that, you will give us the strength we need to push these thoughts away before they have a chance to imprison us in a dark and depressing state of mind.

My Prayer

Dear Lord, I do not want to be a negative person. I'm determined to break my habit of allowing pessimistic thoughts to take over my life.

I can't always control the thoughts that flash across my mind, but let me remember that I am the one who permits them to stay and take control of my feelings. Keep reminding me, Lord, that with your help I have the power to push these thoughts away before they get a firm hold on me.

I realize that before I can push them away, I have to learn how to recognize them. There are times when I don't even realize that I'm feeding myself a bunch of negative messages and images.

Lord, help me know when my thinking is becoming negative and unproductive, when my thoughts are leading me to more senseless, energy-wasting worry. I remember entire days when I filled my mind with depressing memories of past disappointments and mistakes, when I worried and feared that the problems I was trying to cope with would overpower me. It was like a long horror movie playing in the back of my mind. Was it any wonder that I had trouble trying to get through the everyday activities? I don't recall even trying to distract myself from all those sad and depressing thoughts.

Lord, help me fight against thoughts that bring on negative moods and emotions. Let me know how important it is to protect myself from slipping into this pattern of thinking that is mentally, physically, and, most importantly, spiritually harmful to me. Teach me how to replace depressing and troubling thoughts with thoughts that are more positive and healthy.

With your help, Lord, I will keep a positive voice in my mind always switched on. I know, too, that the more I make use of this power, the stronger it will become.

My Resolutions

Every time a negative thought comes to my mind, Lord, I will not sit idly back and allow it to implant itself. I will draw up my lines of battle by talking back to these thoughts and will use assertive and logical arguments against the dark, inhibiting messages that I give myself. I will say "no" out loud, if necessary, to these thoughts and vigorously push them away. When facing a challenge, I'll think of ways in which it can more easily be accomplished, instead of immediately thinking of how hard it will be to do.

I'll have faith in you, Lord, to give me the wisdom and imagination I need to fill my mind with positive thoughts and images.

Dumping Dissatisfaction

My Understanding

LORD, I KNOW that we can never really feel happy if we are continuously dissatisfied. It seems as if having chronic dissatisfaction is almost as bad as having a chronic disease. But unlike a chronic physical disease that comes upon us unawares, this disease seems to be one that many of us choose to have.

We can find so many things to be dissatisfied with—our jobs, our homes, our co-workers, certain friends, certain members of our family, even the weather. What do we do about all of these dissatisfactions? We complain.

We all know someone who is a chronic complainer. I know a golfer, Lord, who complains about golf days being too hot or too cold, too rainy or too windy. He complains that the fairways are too dry or too wet, that the grass is too long, and the greens aren't well kept. He complains about golfers who don't move fast enough, balls that don't go far enough, and clubs that don't perform as advertised. I often wonder why he would even want to take part in a sport that seems so irritating and dissatisfying to him! I think a simple adjustment of attitude could make this hobby much more enjoyable for him, and also for his companions.

Chronic dissatisfaction is one of the shortest routes to chronic unhappiness. Remind us, Lord, that a simple choice to accept things as they are can go a long way towards increasing our capacity to enjoy things and have a happier life.

My Prayer

Dear Lord, some days I think of many things that lead to dissatisfaction. I call them my "if only" days:

"If only" I could get a better job, I'd be happier.....
"If only" I could afford a new car, I'd be so satisfied.....
"If only" the kids were older and didn't make so many demands on me.....
"If only" I had a bigger home.....

I can dredge up hundreds of "if onlys" that I think would make my life so much happier. Or would they?

I've observed other people who have gotten better jobs and then go on to complain about the longer hours and increased responsibility. I have friends who have been able to buy bigger homes only to complain about the increased upkeep and the added stress of meeting larger mortgage payments. Satisfaction doesn't really last long unless we ultimately make up our minds that we will be content with what we have.

Lord, let me appreciate and be thankful for every little thing that I have in my life.

My Resolutions

Whenever I begin to feel dissatisfied, Lord, I will consider what my life would be like if the annoying things were totally removed from my life. For example, an unsatisfying job versus no job at all, a home that needs repairs versus no home at all, children who give me a headache versus no children at all. Not such a great trade-off, is it, Lord?

I will dump my sense of dissatisfaction and begin to express my gratitude for the things that I have in my life, even those small things that I thought annoying, incomplete, or imperfect. I will remind myself, Lord, that everything need not be perfect to feel contented. All we need is a mindset to appreciate the things that we have.

Sweeping Away Self-Centeredness

My Understanding

BEING SELF-CENTERED is such a negative-sounding characteristic. It's no wonder that no one ever wants to admit to it. Yet, when all we can think of are our feelings, our problems, and how it all revolves around us, we have to admit that we are probably too wrapped up in ourselves, aren't we, Lord?

I know that this is not a good way to live. One aspect of depression is that we get so overwhelmed by our own inner feelings we are unable to consider anything but ourselves and our sadness and despair.

The only way to escape from this obsession with our inner sadness is to begin to look outside of ourselves. Isn't that right, Lord? If we spend more time thinking about other people, we'll have less time to dwell on our depressed feelings.

We aren't the only ones who feel sad. We aren't the only ones struggling with problems. People all around are suffering from some type of affliction or disappointment. People are struggling to cope with things that they also find challenging. We all have friends and relatives fighting some type of illness and need support and encouragement. Many of us have elderly neighbors no longer capable of managing the challenges of old age without help. We know families facing devastating financial burdens, too embarrassed to ask for help.

Let us learn, Lord, to be more aware of the feelings and concerns of others, to notice when they, too, are in pain and in need. We must be willing to share our time, our kindness, and compassion with others and they in turn will be more open to share theirs with us.

My Prayer

I'm counting on you, Lord, to help me find my way out of being obsessed with myself and my troubles. It's up to me to make a true effort to turn my thoughts away from myself and to the concerns of other people, to be more interested in the welfare and happiness of others.

I am often guilty of asking people how they are and then not really listening to what they have to say. Help me to be a better listener. Teach me how to be more aware of the feelings of others, to notice if they are hurting or despairing, or in need of my help. If needed, let me help with their concerns. Let me always be willing to listen to their problems with compassion, to help with their concerns, and to offer support when they're facing a tough or frightening situation. Perhaps I could invite a lonely friend to dinner or care for a child when a parent is overwhelmed with problems.

Remind me, too, Lord, that since I have suffered through a depression and have learned from it, I have a firsthand understanding of what it is like to feel low and despondent. Let me share this understanding with others.

I know from experience, Lord, that offering help, support, and encouragement always makes me feel good. Don't let me forget to share a smile or a laugh with someone else. It always brings a smile to my face, too.

Lord, a day without a smile is a wasted day. A day without a good word, a compliment, or a bit of encouragement for someone is also a wasted day. Help me find opportunities to make others feel good.

My Resolutions

Lord, I will try to really listen to others when they speak about how they feel and what they're concerned about.

I promise, Lord, I will remember to pick up the phone and call family members and friends just to see how they're doing. When I hear that someone is going through a difficult time, I will no longer put off calling them, sending them a card or note of encouragement, or emailing them with a message of my support and a sincere offer of my help.

I will remember to pray for others, Lord, for their specific desires and concerns. I am often quick to promise to pray for others but soon forget to follow through. I will begin jotting these prayer intentions on a card and keep it where I can see it.

Dear Lord, I will volunteer or join a service organization to help others. Perhaps I will help out in a soup kitchen or a parish outreach program or in a hospital or nursing home in an effort to bring joy to others.

Discarding Distorted Thinking

My Understanding

I'VE HEARD THAT PEOPLE who are prone to depression are often people inclined to possess a distorted way of thinking. None of us wants to be guilty of distorted thinking, Lord, but many of us know our thinking is often a bit exaggerated and sometimes even downright wrong.

I've read, Lord, that people who have a tendency to be sad usually have a habit of de-emphasizing the positive and jumping too quickly to negative conclusions, which are often untrue and depressing. Insignificant annoyances become insurmountable problems. Some people make a huge deal out of a flat tire or a leaky faucet, while others take things such as this completely in stride.

Others believe that many of the bad things that happen in their lives are totally their fault and end up with guilt complexes. I have a friend who feels guilty because she thinks she should be volunteering in her community even though she's already overextending herself with the care of a severely handicapped child. Another friend feels she should chair a church committee, even though she's already juggling the demands of her job and her children's activities.

We tend to think that one bad event always leads to another and because of that single event, our lives will never be the same. This one event, we believe, can lead us on the road to being a complete loser. We fail a test, are skipped over for a promotion, or have a personal project rejected; we conclude that we will never again succeed in anything we do.

We must understand, Lord, the many different types of distorted thinking that creep into our minds and affect our moods. We must learn how to filter out all the thoughts that lead to negative, depressing, and often false assumptions. If we pay more attention to how we think, we can get our thoughts onto a more realistic and optimistic track.

My Prayer

I realize, Lord, that I won't be able to discard my distorted ways of thinking unless I recognize just how and where I went wrong. Give me the wisdom I need to be able to identify thought patterns that are twisted, exaggerated, or untrue.

With your help, Lord, I hope to recognize those thoughts that have the power to depress me. I want to stop upsetting myself by habitually drawing wrong conclusions about the things that happen in my life. I remember when I spent three days nursing a feeling of deep resentment toward my husband when he failed to help our son with a science project. We later found out that neither of us had asked my husband for his help. I had jumped to the mistaken conclusion that my husband was not willing to help. I wasted three days being stressed and angry.

Lord, because this has been a habit of mine for so long, it's necessary for me to stop and ask myself if my thinking is on the right track. Lord, help me examine my thoughts and my feelings to see if they are realistic and right.

I need to ask myself if things are as bad as I think they are. Do I feel blue because I am ignoring the positive? Do I usually make something huge out of something that is really small? Am I depressing myself by being too self-critical or by seeing only my negative attributes? Am I able to see a more balanced picture of myself by recognizing the assets that I also possess? Do I remember to give myself credit for them? Am I demanding too much perfection from myself, from others, and from life itself?

Help me, Lord, gain control over my thought processes. Help me steer my thoughts into a more positive and realistic direction. I'm counting on you, Lord, to lead me into a healthier, truer, more optimistic way of thinking.

My Resolutions

Dear Lord, I will constantly be on the lookout for patterns of thinking that are distorted and depressing. I will picture a red warning flag going up in my mind whenever I fall into a mode of thinking such as: expecting disaster, taking on undeserved blame, jumping to negative conclusions, excessive self criticism, and anticipating the impossible.

The instant I see one of these red flags go up, I will change my pattern of thinking into a more positive, uplifting, self-encouraging mode. I will keep reminding myself to exert more control over my way of thinking. When I find that this is becoming too difficult for me to do all alone, I will simply hand this problem over to you, Lord, by saying a prayer asking for your help.

Getting Moving and Doing

My Understanding

I REALIZE, LORD, that one of the best ways for many of us to beat the blues is to get up and get moving. A person who has a tendency to be depressed can do himself a big favor by refusing to sit around and think about how sad and depressed he feels.

Getting oneself moving is one of the hardest things a deeply depressed person can do. When we're depressed, we usually draw into ourselves and can see no incentive to get moving. When we get to that point, we must push aside our desire to stay curled up, immobilized.

One of the easiest ways to accomplish this, Lord, is to start slowly, doing simple relaxing things such as planting a small garden, trying a new recipe, organizing a work bench, beginning an exercise program, or going for a walk.

It's amazing how much we can lift our spirits by getting out in the fresh air and walking. If we walk regularly everyday, many of us can walk a lot of our depression away. Physical activity gives our bodies a shot of energizing endorphins that make us feel less stressed and naturally elevate our moods. We've all heard of a "runner's high" that many athletes experience at the end of a run. That is often due to an endorphin rush.

A study at Duke University Medical Center showed that exercise was about as effective in some patients as medication in fighting depression. Exercise also raises our energy levels and keeps us from becoming sluggish and gloomy. Researchers at the University of Texas found that about thirty minutes of aerobics three to five times a week can relieve symptoms of moderate depression by almost fifty percent. Activities such as using a treadmill, playing tennis, rollerblading, or jogging have the power to put our minds in more positive mood.

We know that our faith in you, Lord, can help us maintain the determination we need to do things that will keep us active and enthused about life.

My Prayer

Dear Lord, I can vividly remember dark days when I didn't seem to have enough energy to do anything. It was really difficult for me to get out of bed in the morning, to get showered and dressed, or to fix a meal. It was difficult to even get myself to step into the sunshine.

But I know that every little thing I forced myself to do, even small things like puttering in my garden, playing cards with my children, taking a bike ride, calling a friend, eventually put me on the path to pulling myself out from under that black and depressing cloud. Lord, don't let me be tempted to just sit around and keep myself immersed in a gloomy and depressed mood. Help me to get myself up and moving in the direction of joy and contentment.

Lord, there are a lot of responsibilities in my daily life that often drag me down. But maybe if I stop approaching them with a sense of drudgery, as I often do, I can make my days brighter. Chores such as housecleaning or lawn mowing can become less tedious if I remember to do them in a spirit of gratitude, recognizing that I have a home and lawn to care for, something a lot of people do not have.

Remind me, Lord, to keep my priorities balanced, to remember that pleasure has just as important a place in our lives as accomplishment. Too often, we don't have the time for enjoyable pursuits. We're just too busy to do things that are pleasurable rather than productive. But it's important—no, it's necessary—that we give our psyches a lift by going out to lunch with a friend, by going fishing, golfing, or by relaxing at a play, a concert, or a movie. We all need pleasurable times to keep our lives balanced, contented, and less prone to depression, don't we, Lord?

I'm counting on you, Lord, to keep me from just sitting around and thinking about how tough and sad my life is.

My Resolutions

Dear Lord, when I catch myself becoming too immobilized, I will get up and move even if it's only to walk out into the yard and pick some flowers or watch the stars. I will get started on a daily program of exercise, perhaps a combination of aerobics and jogging or walking.

I will remember, Lord, that sitting and watching television for hours at a time is seldom a good idea. It can actually promote depression. When I'm feeling low, I will remind myself that I can choose to either sit back and feel sorry for myself or get moving in a positive direction. Lord, help me remember that I have only myself to blame for the choices I make.

When I find myself beginning to go into a slump, I'll put on some uplifting, invigorating music.

Embracing the Bad With the Good

My Understanding

IT'S REALLY HARD, LORD, to love all of life, to willingly embrace every bit of it, because there's just as much bad in our lives as there is good. Yes, we do have a lot of really happy and successful moments. But there are times when life can be very painful, too.

Oh, Lord, it's so hard to go through those dark valleys of disappointment and hardship and fear. But looking back toward those dark valleys is when we seem to learn the most about living. The struggle is what makes us stronger and wiser. We can see examples of this in the many people who, after being devastated by diagnoses of cancer, end up becoming confident, faith-filled survivors who go on to help others with similar serious illnesses. We can also see this in the thousands of people who, after hitting bottom with addictions to alcohol or drugs, find the strength to save themselves and other victims, too. We have more strength inside of us than we realize, and being willing to use this strength inspires new wisdom and confidence within ourselves.

We also have to remember that life moves in cycles. It's like a roller coaster ride, isn't it, Lord? We don't like the down periods, but they happen to be a part of life. If we have patience, faith, and hope, we can move through those darker, tougher times successfully and be ready to enjoy life when it again moves into a happier, more contented period.

Lord, teach those of us who have a tendency to get stuck in the down times how to climb out of them more quickly. Dear Lord, I know there are reasons why you allow us to struggle through painful periods. We can't always see those reasons at these difficult moments. I remember sympathizing with my cousin when his son did not get into the college of his choice. Both he and his son spent the summer stressed out over this disappointment. His son ended up taking a year off school and worked in a social service program, which led him into a completely different course of study and on a career path he now thoroughly enjoys. Lord, time will help us gain perspective on our deepest disappointments. There are times when we must take it on faith that everything in life has a purpose. We wouldn't appreciate the good things in our lives quite as much if we had never experienced anything bad.

My Prayer

Dear Lord, life is a bittersweet journey, isn't it? It's necessary for all of us to rid ourselves of our childish, fairy-tale notions where we expect to live happily ever after. Give me the wisdom, Lord, to accept the ebb and flow of good times and bad. That's what life is all about, isn't it, Lord? It's a journey through both the deep dark valleys and the sunlit hillsides.

There are times on this journey, Lord, when I feel that you let me struggle too much. I remember the year when everything seemed to be going wrong in our lives. I was going through chemotherapy for a recurrence of my cancer. My daughter was in the middle of a divorce and needed help. My aging mother had come to live with us so I could care for her. And my husband had to be repeatedly rushed to the hospital with frightening episodes of internal bleeding. It was one thing after another, one thing on top of another. It didn't seem fair for us to have to go through so much at once.

Lord, I won't always understand the reasons for everything that happens. But I can choose to lose faith and get despondent or to hang on to the promises you made to always help us through our difficulties. Teach me, Lord, to accept the ups and downs of life. Don't let me forget that it takes a bit of both to make things grow and prosper.

Remind me, Lord, that it usually takes the tough and the terrific, the painful and the pleasurable, the miserable and the marvelous to bring about a meaningful and beautiful life. With your help, I can lead a life that is good and faith-filled.

My Resolutions

Each day, I will thank you, Lord, for both the good things and the bad things that happen in my life. If I'm having trouble feeling grateful for the tough and painful things, I'll at least say a prayer, expressing my gratitude and leaving those things I do not understand to you and your wisdom.

I will learn, Lord, how to be more patient during the down times of life. I will focus my attention on upbeat things while I wait for a better time to come along. I will not lose faith in my belief that things will get better and you will help me, Lord.

Cultivating Connections

My Understanding

PEOPLE WITH STRONG social ties tend to live longer than people who are isolated and alone. Researchers have found that socializing keeps us both physically and mentally healthier.

Being social creatures, we all need people in our lives, don't we, Lord? We need people with whom to enjoy and share life's pleasures, we also need them in times of sorrow and disappointment. When life gets tough, we need a shoulder to lean on, a sympathetic ear to listen to our concerns. We all need friends and family to support us, encourage us, and boost our wavering confidence.

When we become depressed, we usually draw into ourselves and turn our backs on those who can help us. Feeling joyless, we don't really want to associate with others. We find it hard to get involved in social situations where others are having a good time. We don't want others to see our low periods. Too many people still think depression is a sign of weakness.

Most of the time, we don't understand just why we're so terribly sad. If we can't understand it, we feel that those who know us will not be able to understand it either. We forget that people close to us are usually kind and compassionate. We don't give them credit for wanting to help. We should be more trusting of others, shouldn't we, Lord?

My Prayer

Over the years, I've learned a lot about the goodness of people, Lord. I look back and I can see how wrong it was to feel that others would look down at me for having this "weakness" in me.

More and more people are beginning to understand that clinical depression is an illness, a chemical imbalance in a person's brain that can make one incapable of dealing with life without some help. But even though we know this, it's still hard for many of us to talk about our depression. I had become so good at hiding mine that even my closest friends had no idea that I was suffering with it.

When I was finally able to discuss it, Lord, I was surprised to find how willing people are to offer their support and encouragement. I was also surprised to discover how many of my acquaintances had also suffered through periods of depression or periods of unexplained sadness. Many could provide helpful suggestions on how to alleviate debilitating bouts of depression and joylessness.

It was a wonderful relief to finally be able to share my feelings with others. I no longer had to hide my depression from my friends. I no longer had to make excuses for not attending social events because of the fear that someone might notice my lack of confidence and sense of despair.

I gradually began to notice and understand, Lord, that when I was all alone, I was much more likely to turn my thoughts inward and become engrossed in sad and depressing concerns. When I was surrounded by friends, I was usually distracted from thinking about myself and my problems. It seemed that being in the company of friends allowed my mind and body to have a chance to relax and even to heal a bit. I also found that discussing my problems with friends helped me to gain a better perspective on things that were bothering me.

Dear Lord, keep giving me the desire and the ability to always stay connected to all the good people in my life, to my family, my friends, and my neighbors, to always be willing to trust in their goodness and helpfulness.

My Resolutions

I will remind myself, Lord, that there are thousands of people who are victims of depression. I will never again feel diminished by having to admit feeling sad or depressed or finding it difficult to cope with life.

Whenever I begin to feel blue, I will reach out with faith and trust to my family and friends. I will make an effort to follow their helpful suggestions. If ever they happen to say anything wrong or unwise in their effort to help me, Lord, I will not allow it to upset me, knowing that their intentions are good and compassionate.

I will attend more social affairs that I've been avoiding, trying to keep in mind that these events often help me overcome depressing thoughts. I'll feel as though I've accomplished something positive by getting myself out. I won't sit at home feeling sorry for myself. That's a step in the right direction, isn't it, Lord?

I will, Lord, join a group whose activities will interest me, perhaps a bowling or golf league, or a political or church service group, something positive that will get me out with other people. I will also consider joining a support group that will help me understand my problems better.

Letting Go and Letting God

My Understanding

DEAR LORD, there are those of us with very specific ideas about how our lives should go, and we aren't happy unless things turn out exactly as we want them to. We have the idea that, when things don't go as we planned, we can, and should, step in and fix everything. With this attitude, is it any wonder we get depressed when we realize we don't have the power to fix everything that goes wrong?

Many of us like to play God. Some of us want total control over everything that happens in our lives. We even want to control the lives of those around us. We often give advice to others and get upset when they don't follow it. We interfere in other people's handling of their problems because we think that our way is the best way or the only way to solve the problem. We even try to change the plans of others because we're not happy with the way things are going. We get impatient with other people and with life itself.

We make the mistake of wanting to fix everything immediately. We forget that life often moves at a snail's pace that it takes time for things to work out. We forget that some problems just don't have perfect solutions. When someone has an incurable illness or is permanently handicapped, we cannot fix or eliminate their problems. We can, however, offer support, prayers, and encouragement.

We must convince ourselves that we cannot control all aspects of our lives. We must realize that the best course is to place our problems in your hands, Lord. But being control freaks, that's usually very hard for us to do. Failing to leave our concerns in your hands, we show how little faith we have in your ability to help us.

I have read that a God-controlled life is a life that is happier, less prone to depression. It seems wise to give the reins over to you, Lord, to be patient and to trust in you.

My Prayer

Dear Lord, I'm ready to admit that I'm not always wise in making decisions. I'm often powerless when it comes to solving problems. I say that I want your help, but because I fail to truly trust in your ability to help us, I immediately plunge ahead and try to do everything in my power to fix things by myself. I don't really want to give up my control. When things don't get solved immediately, I worry and fret and forget to call upon you, Lord.

All through the Bible, Lord, you admonish us not to worry, for you promised that you will always be there for us. You said, "Come to me, all you that are weary and are carrying a heavy burden, and I will give you rest" (Matthew 11:28). You told us that if we have faith like the tiny mustard seed, we will have great power.

I acknowledge that all power comes from you, Lord, but my lack of faith still holds me back and keeps me imprisoned in energy-wasting worry. I asked a confident, faith-filled friend of mine how she manages to get through the tough situations of life without worrying like I do. She told me that when things get too hard to handle, she simply says a prayer in which she hands it all over to you. She then distracts herself by keeping busy with other concerns and relaxes in the firm belief that you will, in your time, resolve the problem or that you will give her the strength to live through it. Oh, how I wish I could do that!

Help me to develop this depth of faith, Lord. Teach me how to be more trusting. I'm willing to learn. I'm determined to learn.

My Resolutions

I will eliminate my desire to control things by telling myself that you, Lord, can fix things much better than I can. I will keep this thought in my mind until it becomes a part of my thinking. I will work on developing patience. With your help, Lord, I will learn how to wait for you to step in and help when times get tough. I will remind myself that your timing is not the same as mine.

When I begin to worry, I will say a short prayer, handing my worries over to you. Each day I will also pray:

Lord, I don't fully understand the road that you've chosen for me to follow, but I do know that you've also chosen to walk down that road with me if I ask you to. I invite you, Lord, to always walk close by my side and share my burdens with me and guide me in each step I take.

In the past I tried to make my life go my way. Today, I will begin asking you, Lord, what your goal is for me, what you want me to learn, what you want me to accomplish.

Lightening Up With Laughter

My Understanding

LAUGHTER IS A GIFT from God! A gift that most of us just don't use often enough.

Remind me, Lord, a bit of laughter has the power to sabotage sadness and banish the blues. There are times when a laugh can get rid of anger, soothe hurt feelings and put an end to an argument. Laughter is powerful.

We've been told that laughter is the best medicine. This makes me think of the writer, Norman Cousins, who deliberately set out to heal himself of a debilitating disease, which his doctors had pronounced hopelessly incurable. By immersing himself in funny laugh-out-loud movies, Cousins successfully cured an illness that conventional medicine was at a loss to cure.

Research has shown that a good hearty laugh reduces the levels of stress hormones in the body and stimulates the production of endorphins, those natural substances that make us feel good and give us a sense of well-being. Other studies have shown that the beneficial effect of a good belly laugh can last up to twenty-four hours. It's no wonder, Lord, many of us like to sit down at the end of a stressful day and relax with a couple of humorous sitcoms. I've heard that one minute of laughter is as good as forty minutes of deep relaxation. Researchers have also found that even forced laughter can be beneficial. Apparently our bodies can't usually tell the difference between a forced laugh and a genuine one. It seems that the physical act of laughing—forced or not—still prompts the body to release the endorphins that elevate our moods and strengthen our immune systems. Even the Bible states that "a cheerful heart is a good medicine" (Proverbs 17:22).

We thank you, Lord, for your gift of laughter.

My Prayer

Let me remember, Lord, life is too difficult to always take too seriously. We all need to try harder to see the lighter, brighter, funnier side of life, don't we? Help me, Lord, to laugh a lot more, even when life is difficult.

I recall how my children and I felt ten years ago when we were all gathered together in the outer room of the intensive care unit of our hospital waiting to hear if my desperately ill husband would live or die. Our stressful vigil lasted two interminably long weeks. During that time we all fervently prayed, worried, despaired, cried, and laughed. Yes, despite the seriousness of the situation, there were times when something funny happened and we all shared a good laugh. I remember wondering how we could possibly be laughing at a time like that. But we did. And it felt good!

Apparently our stressed minds and bodies needed the benefits of that laughter. Life gets so burdensome that we either have to laugh or we crumble. Isn't that right, Lord? Help me, Lord, to see life from a lighter, more joy-filled point of view. Help me to see the funny side of things. Teach me how to develop and maintain a good, solid sense of humor.

When I get too serious and stressed, remind me, Lord, of the many times that our family and friends have enjoyed a good laugh over some past situation that we thought was really devastating or humiliating. I know the passage of time changes our gloomy perspective and makes our more worrisome or disconcerting experiences take on a humorous spin.

Teach me how to be able to laugh even at myself and my shortcomings, Lord. Help me to not take myself so seriously. Help me find joyfulness and peace of mind. Make me wise enough to discover a spirit of fun in everything I do.

My Resolutions

Dear Lord, I will try to develop a lighter, sunnier, more joyful attitude toward life.

When I happen to feel sad, I will avoid getting caught up in depressing, mood-lowering conversations, TV shows, or movies. I will make it a practice, Lord, to surround myself with incentives to laugh by placing humorous jokes, cartoons, and sayings on my desk, on the refrigerator, on the bathroom mirror.

I will try to avoid spending time with humorless people who can pull down my mood. I will spend time with friends who are fun-loving and positive. Dear Lord, I will be open to banishing the blues with a good, hearty belly laugh.

Journaling Toward Joy

My Understanding

LORD, I'VE READ that keeping a journal can be very therapeutic. People who are depressed can get rid of their sadness by writing about their feelings.

Research has shown that those who do written exercises improve their mental health more rapidly than those who do not. Our minds can more easily accept sad experiences and overcome upsetting emotions if we take the time to put our thoughts and feelings down on paper. The act of writing helps us reflect on events, to see them more clearly, releasing pent-up stress and reducing the negative impact of disturbing experiences upon our minds.

I've also learned, Lord, that writing has a similar effect upon our bodies. Research done at the Harvard Medical School showed that when women with breast cancer wrote about their fears and feelings, it actually reduced their pain and fatigue and seemed to strengthen their immune systems. It has been found that writing also seems to help physical ailments such as high blood pressure, asthma, and arthritis.

Some doctors and psychologists have called this phenomenon the "Dear Diary Therapy" and have advised their patients to write in a journal for at least fifteen minutes a day. Doing so helps many individuals get past their traumatic experiences more quickly and also effectively lessens their anxieties.

I believe, Lord, there is a positive power in the act of writing.

My Prayer

Dear Lord, I've decided that I'm going to try to keep a journal. It's certainly worth a try, isn't it?

I believe that I will learn a lot about myself by taking the time to write about my experiences and feelings. I'll give myself a lift by writing about the good things in my life, things that I don't give much attention to. I also might alleviate some of my stress by getting the sad and disappointing things in my mind on paper. Writing about our feelings can also help us to stop dwelling on the past, a bad habit of mine that can quickly lead me into a feeling of depression.

On one occasion, Lord, I did try to analyze my feelings through writing. It happened at a time when I was feeling very depressed. I recall trying to reach deep down inside myself in order to bring out and record all the bad emotions eating away at me. It felt good to be able to express all the fear, anger, frustration, and anxiety inside of me. When I finished, I simply tore my written pages into small shreds and threw them out. I remember feeling actually relieved to get all that garbage out of me.

Another time, when I was extremely sad, I sat down and wrote at length about how depressed and defeated I felt. About a year later, when I was feeling much better, I happened to read what I had written and was surprised to discover how much my thoughts and feelings had changed in that year. It made me realize that I could not only survive sadness and disappointment, but that I could come out feeling better.

Dear Lord, I'm going to do my best to incorporate this "Dear

Diary Therapy" into my daily life. While I'm at it, I'd like to address my writing to you. It will be my prayer time, my time for conversing and connecting with you. I'll be depending on your help and guidance with this project, Lord. Let it lead me not only to a better understanding of myself, but also to the establishment of a better, more positive, more joyful approach to life.

My Resolutions

Lord, I am determined to write at least a few lines in my journal each day. I plan to write about all my sad and bad feelings to purge them from my mind. I'll also record all my good thoughts, experiences, and feelings so I can remember them and treasure them.

I will keep a separate section to record all my "feel proud" moments, Lord. I will list all my accomplishments, not just the big important ones, but also the small, ordinary, good things I happen to do each day. I'll also write down any compliments I receive. Sometimes I'm so focused on all the negative things I think about myself that I tend to completely overlook the many good things that other people say to me.

I will make time to read some of the uplifting things I have written, especially when I happen to be feeling low. Besides keeping a journal, I will also keep a folder filled with inspirational and uplifting pieces of writing. At times I read articles and stories that really inspire me, Lord, and then I totally forget what I learned from them. I will keep these articles on hand so I can nourish my mind and spirit.

Fanning the Flames of Faith

My Understanding

FAITH IS SUCH A FRAGILE THING, isn't it, Lord? It is especially fragile for those of us who have a tendency to face life with a negative approach. Faith is something that has to be used and practiced if it is to remain firm and strong. Just as neglecting to exercise makes the muscles of our bodies flabby, so does neglecting to practice faith make our spiritual muscles weak.

It's not easy to keep our faith strong when everything seems dark and dismal, Lord. When we're depressed, we find it hard to pray. We seem to distance ourselves from you at a time when we need you the most.

There are times when our sadness or depression becomes so intense that we feel we don't even deserve your help, that we aren't even worthy of praying to you. The longer we neglect to pray, the harder it becomes. We just drift away from you. Oh, Lord, it's so easy to lose faith when we don't maintain a close relationship with you. When we don't have you in our lives, we actually forget how to trust in your help.

Deep down we know, dear Lord, that you are always near us, waiting with open arms for our return. All we have to do is to want to walk back into the security of your embrace. No, that isn't all, is it, Lord? We must do everything we can to keep the relationship between us close, trusting, and active.

My Prayer

Forgive me, Lord, for having pushed you away as I fell deeper and deeper into despair. I'm sorry for all the times I failed to talk to you, for all the times I failed to share my life with you. I'm convinced that during that time, you were at my side beckoning to me, holding out your help and hope to me. I just couldn't see that then. The few times I tried to pray, I felt as if nobody was listening. I felt alone and abandoned. But you don't ever abandon us, do you, Lord? It was me who turned my back to you. It was me who convinced myself that it was useless to try to communicate with you.

Dear Lord, I'm ready now—more than ready—to build up my faith, to trust in you. I want to draw close to you, Lord, and establish a bond of love that becomes so strong that I will never turn my back to you again.

I know that this isn't something that can be merely desired. I know that I can't just sit back now and wait for it to happen. It's something I have to work at day after day. Just as I have built relationships by talking and interacting with friends, so must I do this with you, Lord. Why is it that I can share my deepest concerns with other people, and not with you? How can I even hope for my faith to grow when I keep myself distanced from you?

There are times when it's really hard to hold fast to my faith, Lord, especially when I see all the sad and terrible things happening in this world each day—the wars, the acts of terrorism, poverty, the abuse, the injustices. I search for some explanation, some reason for the existence of all these things, Lord. I will, however, make an effort to start believing once again in the basic goodness of life. I will have faith that our world is in your hands—that my world is in your hands.

I know that there will be times when life will be disappointing, but I know that you promised to help us through difficult times. I'm ready to take you at your word, Lord.

My Resolutions

I will establish a close relationship with you, Lord, by spending a moment each morning offering you my day, my chores, my work, my interaction with family, friends, and coworkers. Help me, Lord, make all my words and actions worthy of being offered to you. I will speak to you often throughout the day, even if it's only a small thought, a brief one-line prayer, or a simple acknowledgement of your presence.

In the evening I will thank you, Lord, for all you've done for me that day, for the help that you gave me, for the wisdom, strength, and love you have bestowed upon me, even for all the difficulties I have had to face. I'll thank you for helping me get through all the challenges that came my way.

I will take a few minutes each day to read and reflect upon a verse or two in the Bible. I will spend a few moments in silence, emptying my mind of distracting thoughts and keeping my heart and soul open to your inspiration, guidance, and love. I must admit, Lord, I've always found meditating hard to do. I've often made excuses to avoid it because most of the time I felt I wasn't accomplishing anything. Maybe I just didn't give it enough of a chance. I'm willing to now, Lord—each and every day.

Using the Power of Positive Prayer

My Understanding

LORD, MANY OF US PRAY so negatively that we actually depress ourselves with our prayers. We usually spend half of our prayer time telling you how miserable we feel and the other half begging you to change it all. Not only do we turn our prayers into whiney, despondent pleas for help, we don't believe that we will receive your help or that we even deserve to.

Yet, the Bible teaches us to be assertive and trusting in our prayers. It does not teach us to timidly beg. It firmly and emphatically states that we should ask and we will receive, we should seek and we will find, we should knock and the door to your help and grace will be opened to us (Matthew 7:7).

Even the prayer you taught your disciples consists of statements that are bold and assertive requests: "Give us this day our daily bread," "Forgive us our trespasses," and "Deliver us from evil."

Lord, you really want us to pray more affirmatively, with greater certainty and trust. You do not want us to be filled with doubt, despair, or unbelief when we approach you in prayer, do you, Lord? You want us to declare our faith in your ability and desire to help us and to believe wholeheartedly in our worthiness to receive your help.

When you were on earth, Lord, you encouraged us to pray with so much trust and confidence that we'll actually give thanks ahead of time, as if we've already received an answer to our prayer (Mark 11:24). So instead of apprehensively begging for your help, we should pray with a faith-filled trust and say:

Lord, I know that you are helping me with my problem. I know that you and I together will be able to handle it successfully. I thank you for all your help and support.

Instead of timidly pleading with you to make us wise and strong, we should simply and confidently declare:

Lord, I accept all the wisdom and strength that you are constantly sending me. I thank you for it.

My Prayer

Dear Lord, I will pray the way you taught us to pray. No more whining. No more timid begging. No more despondent listing of woes and worries. No more absence of faith. I will pray with a positive attitude and with an unshakeable faith in your promises. I will pray with gratitude, trusting in you, looking forward to and accepting the help, the guidance, the wisdom, and the strength you have promised to give us all.

I listen to myself boldly declaring all these things, and in the back of my mind, I hear this persistent little voice saying, "Oh yeah? Will you really know how to do that? What makes you think that you're even deserving of all that help?"

Dear Lord, I'm counting on you to silence that nagging, doubting voice inside my head. I'm counting on you to show me how to stay positive, confident, and full of faith in my prayers. Show me how to remove distrust, self-pity, and whininess from all my conversations with you. Let me learn how to fully accept my rightful place as "a child of God," deserving of your love, your aid, and your support. I'm counting on you, Lord, to help me grow in faith.

My Resolutions

I will remind myself that there is great power in positive praying. I will speak to you, Lord, in an affirmative and trusting manner.

Just as earthly parents desire the very best for their children, so do you, my Lord, desire the very best for me. Remembering this, I will always pray with confidence. I will not only pray with faith, optimism, and confidence, I will pray with an attitude of gratitude and joy.

Embracing the Big Picture

My Understanding

SOMETIMES I WONDER why I'm here, Lord. What purpose did you have in mind when you created my soul and placed me here in this place, at this time, in the midst of all these people who are part of my life? What is it that you want me to accomplish?

There are times when I think I can see a plan for my life, when I can see exactly what I should be striving for, what I should be accomplishing. It is all so clear. There are also times when I feel confused and frustrated. The picture is cloudy and hazy. It's then that I get depressed. I don't know if what I'm accomplishing is really important and meaningful.

Do you have a master plan for each of us, Lord? Is there some special, unique mission that you want each of us to fulfill?

Every time I get a precise picture in my mind of what my life should be, something unexpected comes up and my life goes in a direction I don't really want it to. There was the year I had to give up my writing because my four-year-old daughter had to go through a series of painful surgeries and months of strenuous physical therapy. And another time when I had to leave my job to take care of my sick husband.

It's very difficult to get a clear view of my goals when I am so busy with all the tedious chores and responsibilities of everyday living. But I realize that it doesn't really matter if I'm able to see a perfect picture of what my life should be, as long as I'm able to accept each day's challenges willingly and try to handle them the best I can. Isn't that right, Lord?

Keep reminding me, dear Lord, everything I do is special and meaningful to you, even the small, ordinary things, especially if they're done with the right attitude and the right intention.

Lord, you have placed me here on earth to learn, to grow, to give help and support to others, but also to glorify your existence and your presence in this world. Let me remember that no job, no task, no interaction with others—big or small, interesting or boring, enjoyable or tedious—is insignificant if it is offered in service to you, Lord. No act is meaningless if it is done with the intention of making my life and the lives of others easier.

My Prayer

It doesn't matter, Lord, if I'm tremendously successful or if I accomplish great and spectacular things. What really matters is how I meet the challenges that come up each day of my life. What matters is that I accept them with an open and positive attitude and that I handle them without selfishness, meanness, greed, or resentment.

I remember occasions when I resented the time and energy it took to do things to help others. How much better it would have been if I had done it in a spirit of love and unselfishness rather than with impatience and resentment.

I have to admit that there have also been times when I was

resentful of life itself. I really didn't want to be here in this particular life, facing things that I found too hard to deal with. But, Lord, you must want me right here, right now, to do whatever I can to make life better for myself and those around me, to learn what I can from each experience, each encounter, each relationship.

Let me be grateful, Lord, for every opportunity I have to learn, to do good, and to serve you. Sometimes I feel guilty when I don't accomplish as much as I think I ought to. I even feel guilty when I decide to pull back and take it easy.

Lord, you want us to work, to take some time to rest, and to enjoy some leisure. You want us to enjoy our family, our friends, all our relationships, to enjoy life in general, don't you, Lord? When you created our world, you took time to work and time to rest and time to sit back and take pleasure in the fruits of your labor. Our lives should also be like that, a balanced mixture of work, service, leisure, and enjoyment.

I want to feel good about the way I live each day, Lord. I know I can feel good if I face each day with a more willing, more appreciative, and more joyous attitude.

My Resolutions

Whenever I begin thinking that my life is meaningless and unimportant, Lord, I will remind myself that each little thing I do or say or give to others is important and special in your sight. Everything I do can be worthy of being offered to you. Therefore, I will take the time to offer all the work, the pains, and the pleasures of each day to you, Lord. I will also learn how to take pleasure in each of my accomplishments and to be more grateful for my blessings.

I will make sure that I don't defeat myself by setting goals that are unrealistic or unreachable. Lord, you have placed me here in this life at this time and place to do whatever I can to learn and grow in goodness, love, and kindness. I will face my daily challenges with a more positive and cheerful attitude. I will keep in mind that you, Lord, want us to always search for joy in the big picture of life.